Unmasking The

Greatness Within

Written By:

Kaitlyn Young

Unmasking The Greatness Within
by Kaitlyn Young
http://youngkaitlyn.phonesites.com

Independently Published
©2022 Kaitlyn Young
Editor- Joshua Luther
ISBN 9798428508734

Table Of Contents

Acknowledgements

-First and foremost, I thank God for the ability to share my journey and for always leading me to where I need to go.

-To My biggest Rock and supporter, Scott Young, who has loved me in Good times and Bad, and Never gave up on me, thank you! (Our Fur Kids, Rory, Melody, Rosie, and Zola)

-My Whole Crazy Side of the Family: Dad, Mom, Daniel, (Serena, Lucy and Laura) Matthew, (Elizabeth, Hugo, and Weasel) Christopher (Azula), Anna (Katara), and Theresa (Angel).

-Mom and Dad Young, Aunt Pam, Christie (Todd, Danyn, Macy, and Beckett)
And Michelle (Todd, Julia and Colt)

-My llama Mama, Corky, and the rest of the fam: Dee, Dave, Bryan, Kelly and Dan.

-The whole Michigan Jewett Agency for being the first group of people to believe in my potential.

-Ryan Stewman for the programs and the amazing Culture he has created in his group called Apex and my whole Apex Family, Including Apex Accelerators, for being such great supporters and mentors to me!

-Kris Whitehead, Mikala Silvestri, and Stacy Raske

-Mind Ninja Team Members: Wiley McArthur and Joshua Luther

Foreword I: Mikala Silvestri

In 2021 I set a goal to meet more people. Since starting this journey, I've met over 400 new individuals and I'm still counting. It's the reason why I've had the pleasure of meeting and befriending Kaitlyn Young.

As an entrepreneur and business owner on this people-centered journey, I've experienced a plethora of personalities, heard unique visions and seen the values practiced and displayed by others... I've met a multitude of interesting people to say the least.

Of the 400, Kaitlyn is a unique young woman. She's authentic in her words and actions, pours unconditional love into those around her, and is not afraid to admit when she's experienced failure.

What truly builds my admiration for her is her ability to take action from her losses and FIGHT. FIGHT for herself. FIGHT for her family. FIGHT for her friends. And FIGHT for those who feel lost or unseen.

Kaitlyn's personal reflections through this book not only show that some of us are given unfair opportunities, but she demonstrates that no matter the struggle, we can still persevere. We can still get clear on our vision, build something for ourselves and others, and take imperfect action. Our past does not define our potential; Kaitlyn is a living example of this principle.

Now, I've met over 400 people, but there's only one soul with the passion, desire to envision and fight for her dream that's made such a lasting impression. I can't wait for the day that I've met 999,600 more people, so I can not only say- but also confirm- that Kaitlyn Young is truly 1-in-a-million.

Feel inspired & Take action,
Mikala Silvestri
CEO of Let's Learn Tutoring
CEO of Level Up ZYX

Foreword: T. Wiley McArthur

What can I say about someone who has such an amazing energy and ability to focus and create? When I first met Kaitlyn, I knew that there was something special about her.

Kaitlyn has the ability to make all those around her better. She exudes empathy, kindness, and absolute joy.

She has such an amazing light that she had kept hidden for so long. Yet though letting go of all of the masks and by uncovering her true nature, she has metamorphosized into one of the most amazing butterflies of light and amazingness that I have ever seen in my life.

I am so grateful to have her as my apprentice and I learn from her daily just as she learns from me.

There is a lot to learn about mindset. And she has the ability to take simple instructions and make it into something absolutely incredible!

She has awakened her unconscious and now is starting to realize that she is powerful.

I am so grateful to know this amazing light and I can't wait to experience her story with you.

She has come a long way to reveal the most powerful lessons that one can learn. And that is to be true to oneself, to honor the light and the dark and to get the learnings from it.

I know that if you read this book and take to heart what she sends out you will have the epiphanies that can change your trajectory. She is an amazing human being, and I am proud to call her my apprentice and I am excited that she is sharing this with us!

T. Wiley McArthur, The Mind Ninja, Best Selling Author, NLP Master Practitioner, Hypnotherapist and Executive Coach

Forward III: By Kris Whitehead

When I first met Kaitlyn, I would have never considered writing a foreword for her. She's...well, a lady of 5'3" and I'm a dude who's 6'2". She's from Michigan, where the winters are cold, and the summer nights might be colder! I was raised on the East Coast where I think I made a snowman once growing up. She likes Llamas. I don't. She had every disadvantage. I didn't.

She worked at Walmart. I HATE shopping there! You get the picture...

See, I was guilty of judging Kaitlyn. My entire adult life has been committed to helping others overcome adversity, yet...when I met her, I just saw a quiet young lady interested in rubbing elbows with successful entrepreneurs. I didn't understand when I met her that she forced me to evaluate my preconceived notions. Through her willingness to be all of who she is, I began to understand that our core values are the same.

What I came to learn about her, and you will too by reading this book is, she is RELENTLESS!

Yes, we might be different in some ways, but we are MORE THAN ALIKE in all the MOST IMPORTANT ways to create positive change in the world.

Kaitlyn is one of those rare souls who is willing...

Willing to ask the tough questions. First of herself, and then, if you are willing to level up...of you as well. She has unapologetically taken the masks off that society, family, and even SHE put on. Instead of letting the world DEFINE who she is, she started from the foundation and has built a life where gratitude and abundance exist together.

Like all of us committed to excellence, she won't ever stop growing or loving. She's learned that the ultimate power is the ability to CREATE and in so doing, shed whatever doesn't serve. If you allow her, Kaitlyn will show you the power of faith. In herself, in God...hell, even in you.

Through the power of HER story, one where she lets it ALL HANG OUT, you will see exactly what I know about her too. She is a warrior, and her ferocity is only matched by her belief that LIFE HAS MORE TO OFFER than accepting the status quo.

The ability to truly bet on yourself is a rare commodity, not just today...it's always been that way. You'll learn to have the ability to look in the mirror, not accept the reality you see staring you back in the eyes, and instead CHOOSE to lean into your inner guide.

All because a single human decided she was worth the effort.

All because she would NOT quit.

You don't have a book in your hands right now.

You have a guide for the attitude and mindset you MUST ACQUIRE in order to find any level of success in life. My hope is that you will take that as seriously as Kaitlyn has done.

My hope is that you'll skip past the judgment of her sharing her story of hardships and see EXACTLY what I see…

A woman who is living her purpose…

A purpose that will NOT be denied.

Kris Whitehead-

Multimillion dollar business owner,

#1 Best-selling Author, and Coach to the Coaches.

Introduction

First Of All, I want to thank you for supporting me by purchasing this book and deciding to invest in yourself by unmasking your greatness that is hidden within you!

Believe it or not, I have rewritten this book 4-5 times because as I grew, the reason why my story needed to be told, and how it needed to be addressed Changed, I realized it's not about what others think of me, but what others can learn from me!

I finally realized; I was still wearing one of the Masks that I have so admittedly preached to people to remove. I was hiding my true Identity of who I was, hiding out of fear of others not liking who I am!

It wasn't until I became vulnerable and searched for the good in my life, and the lessons in the struggles that I truly understood who I am at my core!

As you read this book, I want you to remember one key thing:

"Even when we hate ourselves, God Loves us."

In the moments you feel there is nowhere to turn, you feel completely alone and are screaming "WHY?!?," God is getting ready to release blessings to you, to show your true purpose to the world, the reason why you were created, you just have to hold on for one more Moment to see it!

So here it is, my journey, the story of a woman who is relentless, and how she overcame her doubts, lies, and fears.

- Kaitlyn Young

Chapter 1

The Beginning of Me

As all good transformation Stories go, you have to start back where it all began.

(At least that's what I have been told!)

I was born in a town called White Lake located outside of Detroit, Michigan to the beautiful family of Michael and Kaye Schasser.
I was the first daughter born to them after having two Sons, (Daniel and Matthew) and was spoiled rotten!

In my first two years of life, my parents were very cautious with me. This was because the only girl in my dad's family, His sister, Mary Beth, died suddenly in her infancy. This caused them to be very cautious with me at all times out of the fear of something happening.

Overall, life was good. I wore all the cute little dresses and bonnets my mom would put on me. I could get my way just by crying a little or acting sad.

At two years old, my parents converted to Catholicism from being Lutheran after my dad had an ah-ha moment with God. So naturally, like any good Catholic family, my parents started kicking out more kids, 3 more to be exact! (Another brother, Christopher, and two Sisters, Anna, and Theresa!)

Life in our house, "The Box" as we called it, was pretty crowded considering I shared a room with my two sisters, and my three brothers also shared a room, but we didn't care.
We all had friends, we older 3 went to the school across the street and would go and play together on the playground afterwards. From the Outside looking in, life was perfect! I mean where else could you find a brother who would willingly play barbie and dinosaurs with you?

Now I know you're thinking, "what the heck does this have to do with unmasking the greatness within?" or "We get it, you had a great life, Gosh!" and you are right, at first glance this seems to have nothing to do with the topic of my book, or my struggles I have overcome, but sometimes you have to set the stage in order to understand the whole story.

You see, all it takes is one moment in your life, especially in your childhood, to set your life on a completely different path.

It only takes one event, one voice in your head, to bring Fear, Doubt, and frustration in, to plant a seed of self-destruction.

Chapter 2

It Starts with a Doubt

Imagine this, I am six years old, Ok? We had gone over to the east side of the state to visit my Dad's side of the family. My parents were going to have a weekend alone for once, so Matthew and I were staying a few days at my Aunt and Uncle's house to play with our cousins.

When I woke up the first morning we were there, I went to give their dog, T-bone, a hug like I had previous times I had stayed there.

However, this time, the dog whipped its head around and bit me in the eye! I screamed like any kid would, and immediately, my Aunt woke up, put the dog in the kennel and took a look at my eye.

Instead of taking me to a doctor, or letting me talk to my mom, she decided I was ok. I mean it only hit my eye lid and I could still see, so therefore I was fine. They told my mom I got hurt but didn't tell her to what extent.

Alas, when I kept asking to talk to my mom on the phone, I was told I could not speak to her as she was too busy, and I was given candy instead. In the background I could hear my younger cousin crying because she really wanted me to stay, and so I did.

After a few days had passed, I was dropped off at my grandmother's apartment to be picked up by my mother. Boy was my mom pissed; she had no Idea how bad my eye actually was before then. (My eye was swollen shut) However, in an effort to not scare me, my mom kept her cool around me, she did not make a big deal of it, and wanted to avoid creating angst against me and my Dad's side of the family.

Side note:(I just want to preface and say I do not blame my mom at all for these events that transpired. She was being a mediator for me and was trying to figure out what to do next to make sure I was ok!)

At the time, because I did not know the full story, my malleable 6-year-old brain took the reaction to the situation as: "Wow, my mom and grandma don't seem worried about me, they seem mad that I caused a scene. I mean she didn't even call to make sure I was ok when I got hurt! I must not be worth as much to them as my other siblings."

It was at this very moment, a seed of doubt that would grow over the years of my life was born.

I started to see myself as less than worthy, I decided I would keep everything that bothered me from that point onto myself, and I started to do my best to not be more of a burden then I already thought I was. Sometimes, it is the smallest things that set us on a path of self-destruction, and many times it is not until years later do you actually figure this out!

Chapter 3

Stories Start to Unfold

Side Note:(As we move forward into the journey, keep in mind the events that transpired in the last chapter, they will come back into play again later.)

At the beginning of second grade, my parents made the decision to homeschool all of us kids due to the lack of faith and increase of drug addictions in the surrounding area school systems. My Mom, being the amazing woman she is, took on the daunting task of homeschooling a 6th grader, 4th grader, 2nd grader, and a preschooler, while also attending to the needs of two babies under two years old!

(I am telling you; this woman is a saint!)

We started attending a homeschool group at Holy Spirit parish where I met two of my best friends, Nicole, and Isaac.

When we were not dissecting fish and frogs, we were playing mermaids, house and capturing the flag at the local park called Indian Springs! I remember fond memories of my whole family sledding down the big hills, taking nature walks, and playing on the splash pad! Again, Life seemed to be good!

Alas, in between the good times, I also remember my older brother teasing me, causing me to become really self-conscious, and influencing me to start comparing myself to other girls my age. With my Dad having bouts of anger, depression and working lots of hours, my mom balancing six kids, and dealing with her own self-worth issues, I felt I needed to help out wherever possible!

When my parents would fight, I would lie to my younger siblings about what was happening, thinking I was protecting them. Instead, I was building a metaphorical wedge that would drive a board between us later.

This quickly turned into me lying and coming up with Stories to mask my real life to my friends, and eventually to mask it from myself. At 8 years old, I started to forget what was real and what was fake. I would spin up stories, so my parents didn't think they had to worry about me.

I painted a picture of being a happy child with a happy life so as not to burden anyone. I remember one time in particular, my parents had gotten into a pretty bad fight. My brothers and I went downstairs with the younger kids but instead of keeping distracted or distracting my siblings from what was happening this time, I started staring off. I began internally questioning myself if the reason my parents were fighting was because of me. I started to imagine fantasies, I pictured a time where life was perfect for my family because I was no longer alive, stressing them out!

This caused me to close off my feelings even more, when in reality, my parents were just arguing about something like money, grades, or family obligations. Looking back now, I realize I was stuck in a world of my own madness, and whenever I was alone, it would hit me the hardest.

To get attention, when I was anxious about being a disappointment, I started to Lie and Manipulate people into believing me. In my head, I needed to be perceived as a well-behaved child, no matter how much manipulation it took on my part.

I was SOOO twisted and broken inside without me even realizing it! In my mind, I was the lowest person on the sibling totem pole, so I could not be an inconvenience to anyone, which meant if I needed to lie something away, I would!

This continued on until I turned 10, when my parents announced we were moving. Little did I know at the time, my life was about to change!

Chapter 4

The Middle of Nowhere

In June of 2006, due to my Dad's job needing to relocate him, we moved to a little town in the Middle of nowhere, called Lake Odessa. I was terrified to move at first, as all the comforts I had known were now located 1hr 45 minutes away from me.

I was nervous, yet excited. I did not want to leave all my friends I had made behind, however, the anticipation of moving into a bigger house, with a larger bedroom and sleeping in a cool bunk bed was thrilling to me.

So, there we were, in the middle of the country, in the land of nowhere with 10 acres for us to run and play around on. Looking back now it seems so surreal! My Dad had been assigned a new job area and was excited about the opportunities his work had given him. My mom had more space to be able to Homeschool and cook, and I was excited to have a closet that was bigger and have a new bed set that was not covered in princesses.

The homeschooling continued for all of us, except for my older brother Dan. He went to Lakewood high school because Dan tended to be a very energetic kid and my mom just didn't have time for his teenage craziness with already homeschooling five other kids.

After a few months, my brother brought up a promise my dad had made to him. He was told that if we ever moved, we could have a dog! A little after this, Jack the puggle became a part of our family. From this point, we even began to add a few stray cats to our Home as well. In no time at all, we went from a family of only one guinea pig and a cat, to a family of 4 cats, a guinea pig, and a dog!

As life began to settle down, and the Anxiety of so many changes in my Life began to dissipate, I started to notice, slowly but surely, my good old friend, doubt was showing up again. I went right back to my habits of lying and manipulating.

I started asking myself questions out of fear saying "what if the new homeschool group doesn't like me? What if I don't do exactly what my parents expect of me? What if I don't get good grades?"

Luckily, I was able to fight these thoughts a little easier at this time in my life. I attribute this to the fact that I had a strong faith in God, as I was blessed to have been raised in a very Christian based household. My parents taught us: "no matter what was thrown at us, God had it handled, as long as we believed in him, we would be ok." So, I clung onto that. Thankfully, not long after my doubts had started to reappear, I was introduced to my best friend in the Whole world, a llama who got to know me better than most people, Madori.

Chapter 5

Corky and her Llamas

After a few months of living in our house in Lake
Odessa, a kind lady knocked at our door. Naturally,
my Mom opened the door to answer. This lady,
Named Corky, asked if we were missing a cream-
colored fluffy dog. She had found this poor little girl
wandering on her large property, and seeing as we
had just recently moved in, she wanted to make
sure that the dog wasn't ours.

Of course, my mom said "No, the dog wasn't ours."
However, as they got to talking, we quickly
discovered Corky owned a herd of llamas at the
property behind us! My brother and I, being huge
animal lovers, began to immediately beg our
parents if we could go up and pet the llamas,
especially since there were never llamas anywhere
where we had lived previously.

Corky laughed and said we were welcome to come
up at any time and give the llamas treats. A week

later, my mom and us kids went up to the llama pasture behind our house to visit all these beautiful creatures, these llamas. The llamas were all so friendly, they loved the carrots and animal crackers we had brought with us, and absolutely loved being petted on the neck and back! It was a magical experience for me for sure!

A few days later, while we were working on some projects back at the house, my brother and I were invited back over to walk some of the llamas. Being over the moon excited, we raced up to the barn, where Corky had a llama named Omajache out for Matthew to walk and I was given a llama named Madori.

The first time I looked into Madori's eyes, I knew I had just found my safe place, I had found someone I could trust completely, who would never judge me or tell others my problems. Little did I know, Madori had previously had her own set of issues.

When she was born, she had a leg deformity, and because of this, she had to have her leg straightened on a table every day as she grew up to fix the issue. So, when I was able to give Madori a hug and she hugged me back the first time I was with her, Corky was completely Shocked!

I attribute this to Madori sensing my fear and vulnerability from the stuff I was hiding from others, and that she knew I wasn't going to hurt her. It was SOOO weird, but so life-altering. I felt like I could trust her immediately and wasn't scared of her. Little did I know how meaningful this connection was.

I had no idea that this was just the beginning of one of the most meaningful relationships in my life. I had no idea that this relationship, which was just beginning to bloom, would become my whole world.

Chapter 6
The Llamagirl Competes

From that day on, I would go up to the llamas, put Madori's Halter on her, take her on walks and train her. As time continued, I developed an even deeper bond with her, and after a while, I was even able to pick up Madori's feet that she was so sensitive about!

My brother, Corky, and I started to attend llama shows with Showmanship, Pack, Public Relations, and obstacle classes that we could compete in. I remember Corky creating different jumps, tunnels, stairs, weaves, and many other obstacles for us to practice with. We began to work consistently to prepare for the shows.

At first, Madori was stubborn with the training, and I really believe it was just because it wasn't her idea. However, with love and some animal crackers she would basically do anything for me.

I still remember my first llama show very well. I had no clue as to what I was actually doing, but I remember being so proud because I had gotten fifth place out of ten other people competing in my class! It was the first time I had ever received a ribbon or felt good for really achieving something on my own! At that moment, I swear I was the happiest girl Alive!

Unfortunately, after a while, my good ole dark side started to kick in. I began getting more competitive, anytime I wouldn't place in my class or only place in the top three and not first, I would beat myself up for it.

This goes back to that event with the dog when I was six, I thought I had to be the best to earn my parents and other people's attention. If I was failing at anything, I was failing them.

Luckily, I ended up realizing I couldn't control everything. You see, if Madori taught me anything, it was that if she decided she was not going to do something in the showring, then there was nothing I could do to change her Mind!

I called these little tantrums her 'tude. (attitude) she would pull these moves on me right as we would enter a competition, even if she knew how to do the Obstacle or the event! Instead of getting upset at her, initially, I'd get mad at myself. As a young kid, I didn't Understand or like that there were some things I couldn't control.

This taught me a lot of patience over the years and believe it or not, Madori's attitude became one of my favorite things about her. She also had a love for being the center of attention and getting her diva on. As a result, she ended up in the Lansing State Journal multiple times, along with other publications. To see her being so good and in her element, always made my heart happy.

Looking back, there were so many happy moments caused by this llama, and I now know for certain it seriously kept me going throughout my rough years.

I will never be able to say how truly grateful I am to God for placing Madori, Corky, Dee, and the rest of the farming gang in my Life.

Especially with all the help they provided when my brother decided to get into raising farm animals.

Chapter 7
The Farm Boy

In 2008, my oldest brother Dan was concentrating on track, cross-country, and going to college. He was never really an animal person growing up. However, my brother, Matthew, wanted to take our pet ownership status to another level.

As a result, He entered the world of breeding sheep! Down the road, Corky, the llama owner's sister, Kelly, had a sheep that had rejected her two lambs, so she offered to give both lambs to Matthew to bottle-feed!

Every day (and Night) Matthew would bottle-feed Herbie and Maple, and sometimes I would volunteer to help too. As these lambs grew, so did the farm. Little by little, Matthew would add new species of critters and different breeds of sheep. What started as a small hobby farm turned into a real animal breeding operation!

After my grandma passed away, my brother adopted 2 pregnant pygmy goats for my mom to assist her during the difficult time of losing her own mother. They were the perfect pets for her during this time as they cared for my mom dearly, and she loved them in return.

As Life went on, Matthew got into raising chickens, turkeys, and ducks with my youngest brother Christopher. Personally, I found the birds to be stinky, messy creatures and only became interested when butchering time came.
My brother and I learned how to butcher and prepare the chickens, ourselves and he would sell them to local friends and neighbors to help pay for things on the farm.

Helping Matthew with the farm duties and seeing him work so hard, it really taught me a lot about responsibility. It taught me a lot about perseverance and made me realize what it takes to be a leader to a group of others who depend on you.

I began to notice quickly, that the animals we tended to, became part of what I called "my safe zone". I felt secure being among the sheep and goats, to be among the llamas and to know I wasn't being judged by them. Being around all the animals gave me purpose and goals to look forward to, when I assumed I didn't have anything.

Alas, as I grew older, as time passed on, that negative voice that caused me to doubt myself originally, grew even bigger. After a while, I was no longer able to ignore the negativity.

I started to ask myself questions such as "What else can I do to give myself a chance to be worthy?

How could I resolve the problems I created?

What lie could I tell to make the years of disappointment disappear?

When will I no longer be a burden to my family?

Chapter 8

The Beginning of the Dark Ages

Around the time I turned 13 or 14, I started having a real problem with binge eating. I would sneak into the cupboards at night when my family was sleeping, I would sneak snacks during the day while my parents were busy, and without even thinking I would turn around and lie to my mom right in her face about it when she questioned me.

Every time, I would attempt to convince her that it wasn't me, and when I couldn't do that, I would make up a story so I would not get in trouble. The eating got so bad that I literally turned into a sugar addict. Stealing food became second nature.

I would do whatever it would take to comfort myself with just a little bit of chocolate, a little bit of frosting, or taking whatever, we had in the house just to get a little bit of that sugar buzz. One time, when I did get caught, I remember wanting to run away, I remember just wanting to hide because I felt like I had let my family down.

I felt like an overweight monster who couldn't control herself like the rest of the kids.

Sadly, this was a feeling stuck with me for a LONG time. I was so damaged inside, and I had no Idea why! One of my lowest points I had was when I was 14. My Mom told us she was going through a miscarriage with our brother, Dominic Rose.

I remember going to bed that night, praying ever so hard for God to take me to heaven, to end my life while I slept, and give my parents Dominic so they had a child worthy of love.

I even gave my mom a holy card with the patron saint of Miscarriages, Catherine of Sienna on it hoping it would help God to listen to my prayers. I didn't want to live this kind of life, this madness, my mind had created for me, but I was never going to tell that to anyone.

I had gotten so good at wearing a mask of the happy go lucky girl, that I didn't even know how to handle the hard stuff anymore. When the floods of emotions would get to be too much, or one of my family members would say something hurtful to me, I would run up to the llama pasture, and find Madori. You see, this llama was not only my best friend, but she was also my built-in therapist. Madori knew when I was really upset.

She would let me hug her and cry it out. I would tell her EVERYTHING. You see, I knew that she would not tell the rest of the world my deepest darkest secrets, and to her, I felt like I truly mattered!

(Just a reminder: this was all in my head; my mind was processing everything based on that event with the dog when I was six. If I would have opened up about everything to my parents or siblings, life would have been much easier for all of us, I was just so twisted in my mindset, that I could not see that!)

As my bad habits continued forming, I noticed I was gaining more weight, and I was disgusted with myself. This Caused me to start hurting myself. I thought If I caused myself enough pain, I would be able to discipline myself to stop eating so much. So, I began to cut my arms and blame it on cat scratches, farm accidents and other various things.

When my arms started to look suspicious, I turned to my lower abdomen, and began slashing away at it, when that wasn't good enough, I started stabbing my inner thighs. This quickly became another full-blown addiction for me.

By this time, I had completely lost sight of the person I was capable of being. However, like God does, he intervened before anything got worse. When things had become unbearable, I was introduced to a retreat for teenagers called Antioch, a two-day Catholic Youth Retreat that was centered around teaching youth about faith, ways to cope, relationships and being part of a community.

The second night at Antioch, there was an opportunity to get prayed over by some of the leaders. As soon as one of the prayer groups was available, I went up to it. Instead of asking for help for me, asked for prayers for my family, and the things they were struggling with. Like I said earlier, God knows what we need. I firmly believe he used these people to address the issues in my heart.

These people started praying about things I had never told anyone, and I started to cry! I felt some relief for the first time in a long time. Possibly ever! I immediately became involved in helping to run these retreats, and each time I attended a little bit of my load I carried would fall away, making life a little more bearable.

I attribute my staying alive during this phase of my life to the handiwork of God, through the Youth Director that ran these events, whose name was Sue.

Her and the team she put together for these retreats helped me sooo much!

However, if there is one thing I have learned about depression and anxiety, is that once you start taking some of the layers of the mask you wear off, the rest of the layers become tighter to your face. They start to suffocate you as you begin to realize all the damage you have done.

For example, I started taking every little remark anyone would say about me, personally, and I began to interpret every negative comment made towards me as true.

Unfortunately, in between the awesome retreats, this mentality that my mind had created would cause me to lean back on those bad habits I mentioned earlier. Fortunately, God saw something bigger in me, something brighter, and was not about to give up on me…

Chapter 9

Rollercoaster of Emotions

In the year 2012, My parents and some friends of the family found this place in Ohio for us to all vacation at in the summer when I was 15. The first year we attended was a lot of fun, and I did learn some stuff, but the year I turned 16 was when Shit got REAL!

There was this Dude Named Justin Fatica who spoke to us teens, and man, this guy had a way with words! This guy was one of those inspirational "in your face" speakers. The way he talked made you literally wake up from the false world you lived in. He gave us kids hope that we could truly make it through whatever is thrown our way.

Lastly, he made sure to meet people where they were at, so he could then take them to a place of things becoming possible again! The night after his last talk, I actually felt comfortable enough to disclose to my two friends that were with us. I told them about my cutting, my suicidal thoughts, and my eating issues.

I actually ended up staying with them for the rest of the event. This was due to the fact of the rest of my family having to leave earlier than expected, as my mom broke her leg pretty badly on a hill. My parents were ok with me staying behind to have fun and learn more about my faith.

I was ecstatic about it too as I thought that I had finally found a rainbow bridge. A place that would give me relief from all my baggage, from the masks that were glued to my face, that it would all finally come off. For a while, when I returned home, things were good! I even spoke to my parents about the self-harm problem I had, I even showed them some of my journals I had written in that explained some of my Suicidal thoughts.

Alas, I still did not disclose everything. Something I know now, looking back is when you put so much baggage in the back of your mind over a long period of time, your conscious mind cannot keep up with releasing all of it on its own. Unfortunately, even though I made huge strides in the right direction, my subconscious was still operating like the self-doubting six-year-old, and I didn't even realize it!

Between Catholic family land and the Antioch retreats, I was able to make the decision to stop cutting, and for a while I was eating better too. I enrolled in a program with my parents called "the light way" where you eat just a cup of food at specific times of the day.

I had myself and everybody convinced I was doing better. However, there was still this dark piece inside me that I was avoiding, and I didn't even realize it. This was the piece I had only told my llama about because she couldn't talk back and tell others.
She couldn't tell people, secretly, that I didn't plan on living a long life, that I had always assumed I

would mess something up, I would become a burden, and I would end my life before I hit my mid 20's.

My oldest brother, Dan, sensed that there was something still going on with me, and because he didn't know how to help me, he started to criticize me. He began to tease me about my weight, he would poke fun at what I ate, and how I ate. It got to a point that I would always feel like complete crap!

Looking back, I know that's not what he even remotely intended to happen, all he wanted was for me to have a wakeup call and get better. Dan didn't want me to go deeper into the darkness and deep down I think he was scared to lose me. Unfortunately, even though he had the best at heart, this caused me to spiral even further out of control. I remember one time after him saying something I literally went up to the llama pasture and cried with Madori.

Overtime, I started clinging back to my lies and masks of deception. I was quickly spiraling towards the bottom, and asking myself questions such as:

"What is the point of living?

Why am I even trying anymore?

What am I even going to do after high school?"

This brought me to deciding that I needed to keep people believing I was okay, because I didn't want to burden anyone else with more pain than I already had. I had just to make sure I convinced them I got better, and so the masks started going back on.

(Side Note: Looking back now, as an adult, I know that my brother, Daniel, cared more for me than most humans care for their siblings. He was still young and learning to communicate his fears and concerns properly. I forgave these miscommunications a long time ago and am proud of the growth he has had ever since. He is now an amazing father and husband to his family and shows people the proper way to lead others.)

Chapter 10

Adult World, Here I Come!

In April of 2014, I graduated from high school from my parent's home, with my diploma in hand. Immediately after graduating, I did what any good young adult would do that wanted to prove themself, I got a REAL JOB!

Sure, I had worked as a farm hand, and worked as a temp at an organic seed company, but this was the first time I was going through the application process and putting in the effort all on my own! This landed me at good ole "Wally World", the land of "people of Walmart." My plan was to work at Walmart, taking a year off of school so I could earn some money to pay for community college, and go for some kind of career.

I was throwing around Ideas such as being a dental hygienist, a paramedic, or even a veterinary technician. I never got really serious about deciding what I wanted to do as I didn't have enough belief in myself to think about a real future for myself.

A little after I started working, I got my driver's License so I could transport myself to and from work without relying on my older siblings or my mother to get me there. Soon after this happened, I entered a relationship with a fellow co-worker.

Don't get me wrong, the guy was nice, and I knew that he had a good heart, but I didn't love him. However, I figured being in a relationship was normal for an 18-year-old. I was attempting to convince the world I was okay, and more importantly, convince myself that I was okay!

I started to create this false reality that if I stayed in the relationship, I would fall in love, that this guy would change to be who I wanted. Deep down, I knew due to him having some mental challenges, he would never be capable of giving me what I needed, but I kept lying to myself anyway.

You see, he was very unaffectionate, unable to be physical. We would hold hands and that would be hard for him, he insisted on hugs, no kissing. It took me a year and a half to realize that I was wasting his time, not just mine. He needed to find someone that would communicate to him in the ways he needed, not me, who was a super affectionate person.

I remember it was the day after Christmas, I called him and told him I was breaking up with him. At the time, I was planning to move in with my brother and his family in Florida to get away.

Looking back, I realized it was wrong of me to just call him, instead of breaking up with him face to face. I think at the time I was not capable of seeing that he deserved to be told the reasons why it wasn't in person due to me being so self-absorbed with my pity party I had going.

Around this time, I was also dealing with a lot of other issues. My Llama Madori had gotten really sick. We assumed she had some type of cancer, or disease causing her to lose her hair and develop sores on her body.

She was getting weaker no matter how many medicines we tried, or how many times we had the veterinarian out to see her. Not long after came one of the worst days in my entire existence.

I went up in the morning as per usual to give Madori some extra grain and treats to try to get more weight on her, to keep her strength up like I did everyday lately. Instead of playing the game of chase around the pasture that she so thoroughly enjoyed, Corky found her lying in the barn on her side unable to get up.

At that moment, when I took a look at her, I began to realize how thin and weak she had actually gotten. I noticed how tired she was with each attempt we would make to get her to stand. After a few hours had passed,

I asked Madori the most heart-wrenching question.

I asked her, "Do you want to continue fighting?"

I'm not even kidding you guys, with the little bit of energy my best friend in life had left, she shook her head "no." It was at that moment I knew I had to do the humane thing, the gut-wrenching thing, and make the hardest decision of my Life.

When Corky came back to the barn, I asked her to call the veterinarian to put Madori Down.
Here was the Llama, my confidant, my baby, that had supported me for 10 years. The only living thing alive that knew all my secrets, my struggles and pain. She was the light of my life and to know I was about to lose her forever, when we were so connected at every level, was like taking a stab to

the heart!

An hour later, the vet arrived and started the process.

As Madori looked at me while I held her head and stroked her neck, I felt a weird peace come over me. It was as if Madori was telling me "It's ok mom it's ok. I am going to a better place where I will no longer be in pain, you are doing the right thing."

Though that helped to comfort me a little, I still had just lost one of the biggest pieces of my heart. We buried her on the fence line of our property and Corky's, so she was near both of us.

Every time I went by her grave, I'd ring the bell that Corky had put there to honor her. Unfortunately, as the months went by, I started to close myself off from the llamas. Something in me died with Madori, and I just could not deal with the pain. So, I did what I knew best, I bottled up the emotions, the hurt, and shoved them down as deep as possible. I was putting on another mask to cover things up, to pretend I was over it for my sanity, and my family's well-being.

Around this time, I also quit Walmart, for a door-to-door sales job selling AT&T and DirecTV. This made me get into a routine of dressing up nicely. I had to represent the company I worked for, as well as show I was moving forward to my family. I did really well for a while, I even earned leadership rewards for my hard work.

Alas, even though I realized I was great at sales, the company I worked for did not have a proper training structure as well as did not offer help when it came to preparing people for what the job really entails. This gave me a distaste for anything sales related, for a long time. I believed the industry was not a stable way to provide for my life.

So, to get my feet back under me, I decided to

take a temporary position at a cosmetic factory called Amway.

What I didn't know is that this decision I made would introduce me to the most important person in my life. My later-to-be husband, Scott William Young!

Chapter 11

Life as a Temp

While I was working as a Temp at Amway, I moved
into what I called "the scary house" in a little town
called Saranac with my brother, Matthew.

See Matthew is an awesome brother, he is
someone
that I know I can always count on still today.

The thing is, however, the move to this house was
not the most beneficial to me. The reason being,
my brother ended up moving out of this house after
a few months, but I decided to stay behind.

I started smoking cigarettes, drinking regularly, and
I began to smoke marijuana. I had so many first-
time experiences there, I was exploring and
experimenting everything my parents had raised us
NOT to do.

This went on for 4 and a half months until my parents told me I was to move back home and get out of that house, as they knew it was not good for me.

A few weeks after moving back home, I went to an event my parents were involved in called Cursillo. It made me realize that I was capable of setting a better example for my siblings. I realized quickly that the last thing I wanted was for them to end up like me! My move back home helped with this for a bit. I spent more time with Christopher, Anna, and Theresa as I continued to work over the next few Months.

Around my 6-month mark of working for Amway, I started to be tasked with the production Custodian duties. I began to notice this cute soft-spoken guy every time I would take the coats up to the second floor to wash.

He was so gentle, and so kind, I was truly twitterpated by him, to the point of being unable to talk! To him I was known as "the shy elevator girl." I think deep down I knew, if I did open up to him, we would end up being in a relationship, and I was scared of that.

A relationship would mean that I saw myself doing something with someone else in my life. However, as I have continued to learn, When Something is meant to be, God finds a way!

In late June I took a look at my phone. This time I noticed I had a message from the guy from Amway on Facebook Messenger. He simply said, "Hi my name is Scott," and so started us talking about Amway. This led to us talking about all the different things we liked or didn't like about working there, our favorite past times and the most memorable movies each of us had watched.

The next thing I knew, He messaged me saying "You know, I love going to the movies, but I hate going by myself, would you go out with me?" I immediately said yes without even thinking about it, and so we went to see The BFG in theaters the following evening. Here is the crazy thing, by the end of our first date, I knew that I was going to marry this man.

This gentleman exemplified what a good Christian guy looked like. He literally treated me like a princess! As the nights went on, we made a point to see each other every single day for 98 days straight. At this time, I had also decided to go to college for EMT becoming a paramedic. But after two weeks in, I quit.

I really stopped caring about everything that wasn't Scott involved as I was in what people call "puppy love". I would do anything for this man!

In November, after only a couple months of dating, the man of my dreams proposed to me in the middle of Corky's llama pastures! This drove me to get a full-time job to help provide for my family at a different factory called "Oliver Healthcare Packaging". Working here was pretty good at first, but as life continued into our second year of Marriage, the masks I had worn started to catch up with me.

The figurative bottle I had stored all my past baggage and emotions in was starting to crack.

Chapter 12

I Now Pronounce You Married!

My Handsome Man, Scott and I were married on April 13 of 2017 in a quaint chapel in a small town called Coopersville. It was nothing fancy, but perfect for us. It was intimate and we had the people we cared about there. We couldn't have been happier. We got an apartment in Grand Rapids; we had our two cats and rabbit and lived a blissful life that first year. (That was, until I miscarried our daughter.)

As life went on, I really got to know Scott and how amazing he is and how blessed I was to be with him. I worked harder at my job at the healthcare packaging plant. Nonetheless, I started noticing the bottle I had packed away all of my baggage in was starting to crack. With each miscarriage I went through, I'd go to a darker place.

I didn't give a crap about my eating. I got to be way

overweight. At my heaviest, I believe, I was about 340 pounds. I had started to act around Scott like I had with my parents. This included me starting to pretend that everything was okay and that I was happy. Alas, you could physically see on the outside with my body, and I could feel inside that I was crying out for help. I was looking for a way to end my pain.

Yet, I didn't want to tell anyone how broken I was, so I kept moving forward. I even got a promotion at my job and had become an excellent manager and a great machine operator. I figured that this was the peak of my life, I was never going to be capable or good enough to do anything else. I Convinced myself that I was worthless, I could never do better than where I was. I was making $18 an hour, was loving the team, and overall thriving at work. I was doing a great job of painting to everyone else that I was okay, or that I could handle anything that bothered me. Once in a while I would get on a diet for a short time, then inevitably fall off of it and gain even more weight back. I would turn things that my family would say that Scott's family would say, or things I thought about myself and twist it as negatively as possible just to add fuel to the fire.

Scott's sisters were so sweet to me as well as his parents. They'd reach out and would never judge me. Same with my mom and dad. Alas, I felt my relationships with my siblings distancing. I felt the judgment from people I knew, and I felt the judgment from myself most of all. We stopped going to church. I stopped really having an active belief in God. All I could do was just focus on going to work, coming home, being a wife, and going to bed. It was all I could handle at this point.

I stopped seeing the llamas. I stopped visiting other people. I cut off everyone I cared about. I even stopped talking to my best friend that I was close with, Jacie, and a couple of other friends in my life. I was so good at lying to my parents and at hiding things (financial, physical, and mental) from Scott.

I just kept it going. I'd become the master at putting on masks to hide my actual feelings. It's not like I knew who I was anyway. I just keep adding duct tape to fix the holes in the masks I wore.

I now know this is not the way to operate in life. If I had only reached out and taken the step to ask for help, a lot of my pain and sadness would have Subsided. A lot of the struggles I dealt with would not have happened. Lots of the things that had actually happened would not have hit me so hard, because my perception would have been adjusted. Unfortunately, I was so far gone that I didn't even know how to ask for help! To make it even worse, when people did offer help, I'd say no, because, again, I didn't want to inconvenience or burden anyone.

This buildup of choices and holding it all in kept going until later in our second year of marriage. The figurative bottle broke, the Masks began to choke, and my mind was no more

Chapter 13

I Don't Want to Live Anymore

In spring of 2019 I completely lost it, I came to the
conclusion that I was done living. We had
miscarried again, I was fat as hell, and was
convinced I was just a burden to all of the people I
cared for. I twisted this in my mind to the point of
believing that God wanted me to give up, that
these were signs from him to end my life.

So, when Avenger's endgame came out, I saw this
as the perfect opportunity to say goodbye to those
around me without them knowing it was the last
time, they would see me. I had it all planned out,
we would go see the movie Sunday night with my
side of the family, and I would say my goodbyes
for the last time. Then in the morning, I would kiss
my husband off to work, and once he had left the
house, I planned to swallow all the medications in
our cupboard and peacefully drift off while petting

our cats.

No one would have to deal with me anymore. No one would have to put up with my sad pity party. No one would have to look at the overweight girl that was unattractive. No one would have to look at the human that didn't care enough to comb her hair. No one would have to hear the lies that this woman told herself and others!

The night of the movie, my mom being the smart person she is, knew something was wrong. She kept asking me "What's wrong? Are you okay? Are you sure you're, okay?" Yet, instead of answering honestly, I told her I'm fine, I'm doing good. (With my most fake smile.)

When Monday morning came, my husband realized I wasn't myself. I was acting almost excited because I was ready to be done with the pain. I was feeling relieved that soon I would not have to survive this horrific life that my mind had created for me for so long. Luckily, when Scott looked into my eyes right before he left for work, and asked "What is really going on, Kaitlyn?", the bottle Shattered!

I told him EVERYTHING. I told him what my plan was, how I had manipulated and lied to people, and how I had even lied to him about a lot of things in our life. Firmly believing nothing from this point on would make any of it better, I told him I didn't want to be alive anymore. However, being the amazing person Scott is, He just held me close, and let me cry into his chest.

After a few minutes, he helped me make a call to my parents to inform them I was going to be admitted to a mental hospital called PineRest due to my issues. For six weeks on and off, I would convince myself and the doctors I was fine, and then end up back in the hospital a few days later. It wasn't until one night I had an epiphany. I realized I was starting to put myself back in the hospital, instead of being forced in!

There is a reason I was still alive! If God was done with me, if I wasn't one of his beloved children, he would not have created me or ended me himself! That's why I started putting myself into the mental hospital after a while without realizing it, my Story wasn't over yet. In fact, I knew at that moment, in some way, my story would be the exact thing I would use to help others!

This was just the beginning of me becoming myself. I had removed a layer of my mask once again! I had found a piece of my purpose! Unfortunately, the Journey to overcoming all the years of lying, manipulating, and perceiving I was not worthy of love was not going to be as easy to move through.

In order to do this, I needed to create a safe space in my home that I could retreat to when the urge to relapse came for me. With My husband's help, we took everything out of our walk-in closet. I put a nice chair in there, some soft lights, a fish tank, along with some calming music. I called it my sensory room and mirrored it after the one they had in PineRest Mental Hospital. In Order to distract my thoughts, I made a basket filled with little puzzles to solve, Stress balls, notepads to write on, and coloring books. By having these Items available there, I provided myself with the tools to keep myself out of the deep depression I was so used to being stuck in.

The next step I worked on was developing new habits. The first one and the hardest habit for me, was working on positive self-talk. This involved me daily going into that sensory room and writing out a positive affirmation about myself. At first, I would laugh at the things I had written as I read them out loud, because I did not believe that anything was good about me. Fortunately, overtime, that began to change with constantly committing to it every day.

I began to believe the things I wrote, such as:

"I am strong".

"I'm worthy of great things."

"God has a purpose for me."
 "I am a beautiful human being that is deserving of love."

 "I am capable of losing weight".

"I am capable of greatness."

These were just a few of the many things that I started to believe were true or possible. Once I had gotten a little bit of confidence under my belt, I moved my affirmations to my mirror in the bathroom. This caused me to have to look myself in the eyes while I said the affirmations out loud.

After a few weeks getting back on my feet from

being released from the mental hospital, I was ready to return to work. Nevertheless, I made the decision to quit my Job at the factory as I discovered it was causing too much stress for me at the time. I realized that the work I was doing there was draining me of the little bit of happiness I was starting to get back.

So, a few weeks later, I started working for Walmart again. This time just as a cashier. It was a huge pay cut, but I knew I was making the right decision so I could focus on being the Wife Scott deserved and become the person God called me to be. Each day the more I'd say the affirmations, and the more I would repeat goodness to myself, I noticed the more I would believe it.

After about six continuous months of focusing on learning to love myself, I began to smile as I was reading them! I caught myself one time and let out a laugh saying: "Wow! Look at that, YOU CONFIDENT BITCH! You're really doing it!" Then, nine months of affirmations later, I started to be excited for my affirmation time in the morning. I would anxiously wait to see what I would come up with to write on that Mirror!

At my one-year anniversary, the psychologist I had been working with in regard to Managing The disorder I was diagnosed with, (Known as Borderline Personality Disorder) made the decision to take me off all the antipsychotics and leave me on just one anti-depression pill!

I had finally reached a place with my mental state where I was able to start working on the other things, such as my weight and my purpose.

Chapter 14
The Climb Begins

In March of 2020, I brought home a cute baby puggle-pit (a pug-beagle-pitbull mix) named Rosie. She was the cutest thing to hit Earth and our family felt complete. I had a husband who supported me, a dog that understood me, and my cats who were brats, whom I loved anyway. Unfortunately, however, the day after getting Rosie, I got sick with Covid-19.

My breathing was terrible at best. I was put on covid leave and was in bad shape. Eventually I started to recover, so two weeks later, I went back to work. I had worked half the day and was going to my car for lunch. All of a sudden, out of nowhere, I was not able to breathe! I was on the phone with my mom and dad, while waiting for Scott to arrive, just barely breathing in and out. Once Scott had arrived, we immediately went to the hospital. Alas, at this point in the pandemic,

Covid tests were not available unless you were a first responder or worked in health care. So, like many people at the time, I was diagnosed with probable COVID.

I had to stay for a while unfortunately, as my oxygen had gotten so low (under 89) and my blood pressure so high (over 200), and as a result, my heart had become enlarged. I was given medication and observed, and, because of my overweight nature, I was put on a high alert list (I received an echocardiogram later on and it is now back to normal size, praise the lord!).

I was down for a couple more weeks, but during this time, I removed another mask. I came to the conclusion the weight needed to go. It was at that very moment; I made the decision to get healthy. Yet, how do you even start when you're 340 pounds at 5ft 3in?

Where do you go to get help?

I of course began by looking online, and looked at different diets, fads, etc. I quickly came to the realization that I had already tried all of these things growing up. I knew If I was going to truly change, I needed a solution I had not pursued before. This led me to a consultation with a surgeon about weight loss surgery.

It was decided by the both of us that the gastric sleeve (where they removed 75% of your stomach) was the option for me! After multiple months of doing the work and losing 40 pounds on my own, November 17th, 2020, I went in for gastric sleeve surgery. They put me under the knife and afterwards I came out revived. Immediately, I started walking around the hospital, only 2 hours after my operation! They told me I moved very fast through recovery, and so as such I was released to go home the very next day!

I worked hard and stuck to the Diet. Unfortunately, 3 weeks after my operation, I began to notice my abdomen pain was increasing, which I thought was weird. The doctor that did my surgery, ignored me, and told me I was fine.

Thankfully, God brought some good friends back in my life that encouraged me to get a second opinion. Within a few weeks, the second doctor had my gallbladder and appendix removed on January 5th, 2021. This is when my real weight loss started and another mask, I had worn for so long came off! I ended up getting down close to 200lbs. Feeling better than ever, I was even able to play with my nieces when they came to visit us from New Mexico. I was able to walk and do the hard things I wasn't able to before! My husband and I began to have a much more sexually active life, and our relationship began to grow even more!

Everything was going perfect, I mean, I got a promotion at Walmart, I was a team lead running the apparel side of the store and learning how to do tasks the store managers usually took care of! I got to the point that they would trust me to be left in charge of the store many nights on my own. Things were perfect!

Alas, because I didn't listen to my gut, (a.k.a. God) I made the terrible decision to get the J&J covid vaccine. (All because it would put $75 in my pocket!) Looking back, I had such a small mindset, I only saw the dollar signs and didn't care about the consequences. A month after the shot, I became paralyzed in my leg from a stroke. Just as I was beginning to recover from it, I had another one. This time, my husband found me in the living room, unresponsive, slumped to one side and twitching. He immediately called an ambulance. They came quickly and I was taken to the nearest hospital with a stroke unit.

They administered TPA, a drug to stop the stroke. (a very strong anti-clotting agent) Looking back, I remember my husband being so terrified, and yet, I was not able to respond to him, as my voice was not working. They put me on some other medications, and within 2 days I was back home and seeing a neurologist regularly. On my second visit seeing her, she put me on anti-seizure medication as the last stroke left me with a seizure disorder that occurs if I get too stressed or if I overdo it. This medication helped big time!

Without a break in between, however, I began to have stomach problems again. I was immediately referred to a gastroenterologist after finding colitis in different areas of my digestive system. At the time, they diagnosed me with Crohn's Disease, however as of now I am undergoing more testing to find the real cause.

When I finally got better from everything, I went back to work. However, I quickly realized I didn't belong there anymore. I knew it was time to work on the purpose God had waiting for me, what I didn't know is that this was just the beginning.

Chapter 15
Michigan Jewett Agencies

Once my health got better, I quit my job at Walmart, and joined an insurance business Called "Michigan Jewett Agencies." The Only reason I even accepted their job offer, was because when I went in for the interview, the employees were so happy and energetic. I had never experienced that in a workplace before!

I noticed as well that I was immediately drawn in by the Owner, Deane Jewett. He gave a unique presentation on what to expect working for them. Unlike any other company I had come across, he genuinely had people's best interests at heart.

A few weeks later, I passed my insurance exam, and I knew this was my chance to go all in on my career. Now that I've worked on my health, my mental side. It was time to see what Kaitlyn was truly capable of.

I worked with Lori, and Devin as well as all the other leaders in the agency, and let me tell you, one thing was clear: these guys had a mission to help families, not just numbers. I realized being surrounded by people that were focused on leveling up and focused on helping people, not just on monetary value, was the best decision I ever made!

Right off the bat, they paid for me to go down to Florida to go to a Grant Cardone Conference. This is where I realized "holy crap, I can do this!" Just a week later, Lori, out of the Kindness of her heart transferred ownership of an extra Apex membership she had, to me!

I am still so thankful and grateful for her Kindness, especially when I learned about what apex is all about! Apex is a Family of Choice, a community that supports each other, and focuses on helping you become the best version of yourself!

Looking back, I am grateful my time at the insurance agency taught me the importance of doing the work no matter what came up, and that consistency is key. I thought things couldn't get better and thought that I had just hit the peak of my life! (I was happy remaining behind the masks I had left to remove, and at the time I didn't even know they existed)

Each Monday, When I would go to the office early and excited to learn from people such as Deane, Lori, and Devin, I was taking as many notes as possible. My unconscious mind was looking for the answer to my purpose in all the weekly discussions we had, The Leaders of the Agency taught us how to become our best selves, how to invest completely in the job while taking time for you, how to hit your weekly goals, and lastly how to close the sale the correct way.

I became so inspired, which led to me coming up with an idea called Llamaland. At first it became just a llama center that would be attached to an amusement park, then it was a llama farm that people could come visit, and lastly, it was a retreat center with llama therapy included. The vision that had was growing and kept getting bigger and Scarier.

Yet, these people supported every last part of me being "the Llamagirl". The agency had my back, they knew what I was capable of and invested in me, even when I didn't know what I could do myself!

This all led to an event in November, called Apex Live. What I did not know was by going to this event, the masks that were left would come off quicker as time went on.

Chapter 16

Apex Live and The Mind Ninja

In early November, my husband and I flew down to Dallas, Texas for an event called Apex Live. As if going to the event wasn't cool enough, I had also got nominated for an award after only being part of the Apex for 9 weeks! The nomination was for up-and-coming Apex members in the category of Posting and Content, and man was I honored! Considering that Apex consists of over 1500 badass business owners and entrepreneurs that dedicate themselves to becoming the best version of themselves, doing the work no matter what, and representing what winning looks like in their daily lives, I was in awe.

I remember being so excited and thrilled that I was about to meet the amazing people that I had met online in person for the first time! I knew in my heart, going to Dallas would change my life, I just had no idea how much! That morning of the event, Scott and I arrived at the hotel where it was being held, and let me tell you, there was a new and different feeling I experienced when I walked through those doors.

I quickly realized that this was not just some group of entrepreneurs who win at life, this was a group of people that completely supported each other. This was a family who wanted the best for one another and would go the extra mile to help their fellow Apex brothers and sisters out!

I began to notice that they clapped for each other when someone published a book, they cheered each other on when someone made a sale, and when you crushed something in your life, they called it ringing the bell!

It was at this event, I realized, that the creator of Apex, Ryan Stewman, had developed something way beyond the course I thought I had gotten. He had created a beautiful and life changing Family of Choice, a group of people who would never give up on you as long as you NEVER stop doing the work!

While In Dallas, I got to meet "The Mind Ninja," Wiley McArthur, in person. You see, I knew Wiley was cool, as I had the privilege of talking to him a few times. However, when I saw how much Scott was learning from him at Apex Live, I knew I needed to find out more about him.

I began to learn that Wiley was not only an Apex executive, but also a Master Practitioner in Neurolinguistics Programming who coaches people to become their most magnificent self. Later On, when Wiley asked if I would like to join his 8-week Program that he was starting, I immediately said yes! Before I could even blink, the next thing I knew, Wiley was installing these things called anchors on me.

I had no idea what an anchor was until then, but thankfully he explained that an Anchor was a spot you pick on your body and when it is touched, it would immediately bring up the emotion that Wiley programmed to it. So, for me, my spot became the tattoo that I have on my right arm, my butterfly. This is because my butterfly (with a semicolon in it) represents that my story isn't finished yet. So, when I press it, I can access 5 different emotions to help me, depending on the situation. It's a very powerful tool that, before Wiley, I didn't know existed.

After seeing the results from this, I became sold on what the Mind Ninja was about!
Seeing how this changed my life as well as Scott's, brought me Closer to the removal of my next mask. One that was hard at first to let go.

However, If I have learned anything from my past, it's that: "when God is calling you Jump, you better up and Leap!"

Chapter 17

The Change in Directions

We got back from Apex live and of course, I was motivated as ever to find my way to make a difference in the world. I was so inspired that I even agreed to be on Clint Riggins "Limitless" podcast. At first, I was terrified of the idea, especially because I just had emergency surgery to remove a big hemorrhoid. (TMI, I know. lol) However, something inside me knew that my story needed to be heard.

I was so proud of the podcast when I was finished, as was my husband and Clint. Other people, however, were not so happy. They believed that I was telling things that were private, or didn't do certain parts of my story justice, this caused me to get really self-conscious. Some even thought that by me always talking about my family of choice, a phrase we use in Apex all the time, that I was disowning my family of blood. This was very far from the truth.

There was a separation that happened between different people that I had known. I started taking things way too personally and beating myself up again.

I knew my story would help people, but I didn't want to hurt those that were involved in it. I knew that I was called to give my light to others, but I didn't know how to do it without hurting the ones I loved. This caused me to reach out and call my coach Wiley MacArthur.

We talked through the situation, and he gave me different mind hacks that would help. We talked about how looking at things from the other person's point of view would help me get some insight. As usual, he was right. I was too concentrated on "Woe is me!", "They don't like me!", "They hate my beliefs!", "Bla bla bla bla bla!" In reality, I cared too much about what they thought, instead of caring about what was true and needed to be said.

One of the things I've learned as I have grown is that you have to be authentic in your story. You have to be able to say the hard things that might piss people off, because that's the only way you're going to truly help others. As time went on and I began to change even more into the powerful person God called me to be, Llama Land started transforming into this bigger idea.

I noticed I had a calling to step out of "the Llamagirl persona" and step into something bigger. The problem was, I did not know who I was without being known as "The Llamagirl". I still wasn't clear on my true purpose and was still hiding behind a mask.

I knew that I needed to take another step to becoming the person I was destined to be. So, I agreed to a process called a "Negative Emotion

Clear" that Wiley offered. Basically, in less than two hours, I had let go of all my baggage. All the times I hated myself, all the time that I had second guessed myself, and all the times I held onto the feelings of my doubt of worth ... gone. All the years I had tormented myself with guilt, anger, sadness, fear, and pain were wiped clean. I had finally let my past go.

The best part was I still had the lessons I learned from all those experiences attached to the past, just no negative emotions.

I remember crying happy tears for a while afterwards because I had never felt so light. I had never felt so clear on which path I was destined to take next. I knew that the insurance agency was no longer where I was called to be anymore.

Alas, I didn't jump the gun right away.

I knew that I had a huge purpose that God had just started to ingrain in me. I knew that I needed to use my story and use the things I had learned from my past to help others but had no idea where to begin.

All I knew is I needed to be involved with the work Wiley was doing.

The way he was helping people kept calling at me.

Each day this calling got stronger.

It quickly got to a point I knew I could not ignore it any longer, so a few days later, I sent Wiley meme that said "Son of a bitch, I'm in."

He said, "In what?"

I said "I don't care If I have to clean your toilets, I don't care if I have to do the lame crap, but I want to work with you. What you do and how you help people inspires me greatly and I know this is where I need to be."

And with that he said, "Okay, we'll figure it out."

In that moment I knew by putting myself out there, I had just removed another mask, the layer that liked to keep me quiet and small.

A little while later, on December 14, 2021, I officially turned my two weeks' notice to the amazing people at Michigan Jewett Agency and started to work towards the dreams and goals that were set before me.

It was also around this time that I joined Apex Accelerators, which was created to help fellow Apex Members build the processes out for their business.

Chapter 18

Apex Accelerator

In mid-December, I had signed up for a two-hour call with Kris Whitehead to learn more about a group called Apex Accelerator with some other Apex members. Here is the crazy thing, Kris never had to make a pitch or truly try to sell the program. The testimonies and stories of growth that were told during that call sold themselves. When you see grown men cry because they truly found themselves for the first time through said program, you know something is legit.

However, I had a problem. I was $200.00 short of the price I needed to join, and the money I had at the time was supposed to pay my bills for January. I had a choice to make.

A. take a leap of faith and trust God would provide and overdraft my account.

or

B. Say no and possibly let the very thing I have been searching for pass me by.

Without a second thought, I over drafted my account. All I can say is something had pulled me deep inside and told me that this was the right choice to make, somehow, I knew this was where I would get the tools to truly uncover what I was capable of.

I'd learn how to get the most out of Apex, and to truly step into my purpose!

The first assignment we were given the following week was a series of videos called Activating My Purpose (AMP). Through the videos, we learned all about creating a "I am statement."

Something you put together to really capture who you are, your purpose and where God has you. I will be honest; I didn't nail it the first couple times. However, on the third time, I had finally nailed it for where I was!

This statement not only opened up my eyes as to where I want to be, but WHO I was MADE to be! My passion for helping others and assisting them in becoming their best selves, was no longer hidden. I was finally able to remove this layer of the masks I wore, by going all in on working with Wiley.

At the end of December, I began working for the Mind Ninja Full time as the Mind Ninja Apprentice, sales, and customer service Manager. As we began growing the community and put more focus on people we were helping, we also got focused on the direction we were heading as a company.

I also began to spend more time working on my

personal development. This Included me reading more books that would assist me in becoming a better servant to others, and to help me get a better idea on who I actually was.

I learned so much from Authors such as Stacy Raske, Jessica Dennehy, Jennifer Carrasco, Tomas Keenan, Kris Whitehead, Drewbie Wilson and Ryan Stewman. I realized to become who I was called to be, I had to fully surround myself with people that believed in my mission, who believed in my passions.

My husband started to notice a transformation taking place within me since working with Wiley and joining Apex Accelerators.

He was inspired by it so much that he signed himself up for a negative emotion clearing with Wiley on his own.

You can learn about Apex Accelerator by visiting:

https://ee289.isrefer.com/go/AA/a59/

Chapter 19

Growth Happens

On December 30th my husband, on his own, signed up for a session with Wiley to let go of the negative emotions from his past. Now bear in mind my husband is an angel and is perfect in my mind. However, the transformation I began to see in Scott immediately following his negative emotion clearing was absolutely amazing.

I saw the person I had grown to adore, and love be transformed into a more confident and able leader. I saw someone who always doubted his worth, rise up and own the greatness within him. It made me tear up that he finally had relief from the anxiety he always battled. I also noticed our communication abilities improved; we were more open to each other than ever before! We started to laugh and smile more and became completely on the same page to what the other was trying to say.

Our love for each other has grown deeper. (I didn't even know that was possible because I loved him so much already!) This was just the beginning, since that day, we decided that the next move for our family would be to move to Texas in August of 2022. That way we can move and be closer to the apex community, to be closer to one of my best friends Jesse, to Scott's sister Michelle, and truly start anew as the power couple I know we are!

Every day, life has continued to change dramatically. We no longer tolerate people pushing us down, we don't tolerate people treating us less than what we deserve, and we definitely tolerate people who hold our past against us to affect us.

In addition to the growth of Scott and I, "The Mind Ninja Company" began to grow even more. We started to establish a CRM, we set up automations to deliver better service, and dialed in our overall systems. All three of us started to put more energy and focus into what we were doing to help people.

We all knew how important it is for someone to let go of who they were, the fake masks they wore, and to step into their ultimate selves.

The funny thing is at the time I wrote this. I had no idea I still had one more mask to let go.

Little did I realize, over the weekend of February 18th, Llamagirl was about to grow up. I had no idea that I was about to truly step into my purpose and claim the true me that was hidden within.

Chapter 20
Becoming InFLOWential ™

The funny thing about stories is we always think we have hit our happily ever after, and then later on we find that what we really experienced was the end of a chapter, not the whole book! Our stories continue on, and when we are truly in flow, we reach a new milestone every step of the way!

I only discovered this myself, over the weekend of February 18th, 2022, when I truly stepped into Kaitlyn Young: Unmasker of Hidden Truths within stuck entrepreneurs and business owners.

After attending Apex Live: GoonSquad Edition the first week of February and spending my last dime to buy the Premium ticket so I could get a coaching session with one of the members, I contacted Kris Whitehead to set up the One-on-One coaching call with him.

During this Meeting I was able to have with Kris, we talked about various things, some that were hard to hear, and some that were encouraging. I took so many notes and listened to the feedback he had to say.

I realized after getting off the call I had a lot of areas in my development I still needed to discover, but I had no Idea where to even begin as I was "just the Llamagirl."

I had always placed my value based on my ability to accomplish a task for someone above me, and so to think about being my own entity, someone singular and of their own accord was terrifying to me.

After a week passed, I got on a plane and flew to Florida for Stacy Raske's InFLOWential Impact event she was putting on that weekend. I had decided to attend based on how much Stacy's book "Be a Boss and Fire that Bitch" spoke to me, and because my partner Wiley was going to speak on stage. I had no Idea I would be walking out of that event knowing my purpose and who I was!

There were so many amazing speakers, but the most memorable moment for sure was when God spoke to me that weekend. We had just finished a deep breathing exercise, laying down on our backs. I went to sit up, and it was as if the gates of heaven opened themselves. I envisioned a sandy ground for a moment and all I could see were the simple words "unmasker of hidden truths" written in the sand.

It took the whole day for what that truly meant to sink in, but when it did, I could not hold back the tears.

It was at this moment; the final mask was removed. You see, I FINALLY realized the name I had created for myself everywhere A.K.A. "The Llamagirl" was in itself a mask. I was hiding behind my passion for llamas and missing the point God had been telling me all along,

"My story was my path; I was made to break the chains of false Identities and help others connect with their true selves.

I now realize in the past, my unconscious was attempting to protect me from the hurt, it was scared of the unknown, the different and real me.

The Kaitlyn that is Confident enough to accept that her purpose is to help others become their best selves by removing the lies and bullshit they tell themselves.

Kaitlyn, who is not afraid to own her issues, to be raw and real to the world.

Kaitlyn, who never gives in and keeps fighting no matter the cards stacked against her!

After the first day, I remember being so anxious to go back to the hotel room and put all my thoughts down on paper.

To take the tools I had gained from Apex, Apex Accelerators, Wiley, as well as Stacy Raske's event and finally write the I am Statement that encapsulated who I truly was!

I stayed up until 3 am that night writing out my mission statement, rebranding from the "Llamagirl" to "Raw and Real Within" and dialing in my core values for myself and my new company I would eventually Launch. (thanks to Tomas Keenan's book, "Unf*ck Your Business" for help with the core values by the way!)

The next day of the event, I was so pumped, I knew my purpose, I knew my vision, my values, and I knew God had me right where I needed to be, working with Wiley and Joshua.

Over the rest of the day, we heard so many amazing speakers, there was so much crying and healing happening in the room, and we did so many exercises from the talks that amplified and confirmed my purpose.

By the time I came home, I had written this chapter to add to my already finished book.

Like I said at the beginning of this chapter, when you think you hit your happy ending, you really just hit the end of a chapter inside the story, not the whole book.

You have to continue forward and never stop being relentless even when the Force of Average, (A.K.A. life) does everything in its power to stop you.

If you are interested in learning more about Stacy Raske and the group she has, that is Changing the world, Scan this QR Code:

Chapter 21

Perception is Reality

I want to make sure to address that at the time of my childhood adversities, everything was super real to me, I learned everything had to do with perception. A phrase I recently learned is: "perception is reality."

I never really truly understood what this was, until this year. You see, recently I learned my younger siblings saw me as a lying, manipulative person, and let me tell ya, that was a hard pill to swallow at first. Here I am, finally, authentically me finally, not lying to myself or others, helping others become their best selves, and some of my own siblings won't even talk to me.

My defensive side at first said, "Oh my gosh, I can't believe they still see me that way. Look at all I've done to improve blah, blah, blah." But in reality, I had lied to them so many times, I had manipulated them to believe what I wanted them to believe growing up!

Looking back, I now know I started the story telling others to originally protect them from what I was hiding in myself, to make them think that I was the cool sister, when in reality I myself was falling apart. Believe it or not, all I wanted them to do was love me. I would have literally given them the shirt off my back or lived on the street if I knew that it would result in them liking me.

The last time I remember doing this to my siblings, I had gotten my sister a job at Walmart with me. Scared to lose her, I told her "Everything is great, you will only work these days, blah blah blah." And that was not the case. I just wanted her to be near me because I felt that we were finally developing a relationship. I just wanted to see her happy and spend time with her. Instead, what this ended up doing was destroying every ounce of trust we had left from the relationship we were building.

Another example of me doing this was when I was even younger. I would lie and tell them stories to ignore what was going on within me, when in reality, I was really lying to myself I would create these false realities that would bring them into, and it resulted in them starting to question moments in their childhood.

They accused me of manipulating Scott into marrying me. (Which was not the case btw) They accused me of still being fake. Now old Kaitlyn would have taken this deeply and probably gone back to cutting or much worse, thinking she was a burden. However, the Kaitlyn I am today looks at it from their perspective and feels pain for them.

I see their side and I want to make it right. I still to this day have mending to do there, and so I put the ball in their court. When they are ready, I will be here to listen, and hear their side. What happens with that is still to be determined. The point of me telling this to you is because one side of perception is very different from the other.

Here I perceived my past as me being a young girl attempting to survive the chaos of her own mind and the Lies it was telling her, but that does not discount the perceptions of others. When we get accused of something or someone says we did something and we do not remember doing it, we need to take a step back and look at it from a third-person point of view.

Look at it from their eyes. Look at it in a different light. That's the only way you can move forward. That's the only way you improve and own yourself. Now, if you own it and you apologize and you do everything in your power to make it right, that's when you have to let go.

I gave opportunities to people in the past when I shouldn't have and now, I am moving forward as the authentic me by establishing boundaries to know my limits.

When my siblings are ready, they can come to me, and we can repair that relationship.

I will not force them to be ready because I know what their perception is. I'm also not gonna let it affect me every day because I know I'm no longer that person. I know my husband and I are creating new things that are going to be beautiful and are already beginning to bloom.

I know that my life has meaning. I am helping people daily in my actions by letting go of habits that served me wrongly in the past and stepping into my authentic self.

One of my favorite movies that reminds me of this is actually "Frozen II". The reason being, when Ana, after Elsa gets frozen and Olaf disappears, she sings a song about doing the next right thing. That has become the motto for my life. "I'll take a step and then step again and do the next right thing."

Chapter 22

The Work is Required

I wanted to also make sure I address how I let go of the habits of lying and manipulating. I was able to undo the years of habitual and automatic deceiving when I started to read affirmations to myself in the morning and I began to meditate.

I would sit for five minutes and listen to an audio file on an app called Headspace and notice how my body flows as I breathe. This helped me bring focus back into my life.

I then made a point of doing everything with intentionality. That meant before I made a decision, I would think it through completely, Was this process annoying? Yes. Was it necessary? Also, yes! So, for 35 days, because I didn't trust myself at first, I would get my husband's input to make sure that I was going based on facts, not the made-up reality in my head.

I started talking to a therapist and I made a point to put things up around the house that said, "You're enough." That way when I would start to catch myself, (because you do once you really become intentional,) I would stop, and I would apologize. I would say, "Is that right?" I would ask myself, "What would Jesus do?" I would ask myself at the end of the day, "Did I do everything with intentionality today?", and if I messed up, "what are the things I need to fix?"

By doing this self-assessment on me daily, being diligent, and changing how I reacted, I created new habits and removed the ones that were no longer serving me.

I started to time-block my day and make sure that I was using all my time for things that mattered such as bettering my faith, my family, my mission, my knowledge, or my health. I now have people that keep me accountable, and I stick to a schedule daily to help keep me focused as well.

Between these changes and surrounding myself with the right people, I have moved into the most authentic version of me. I will say, the force of average is a real thing that fights us every day and pushes us down.

The key is to acknowledge when it is attempting to push you back to the broken you and fight harder.

It just takes one step in the opposite direction of average every day to improve and become better by 1%. You add up 1% every day and in 100 days you're 100% further in the direction of your goals, and 100 days longer without turning to the habits that held you back.

Only then can you truly Unmask the Greatness Within YOU!

The End Stuff

Resources

Thank you again for taking the time to read my journey and how I stepped into my purpose. Here are some resources below to keep in touch as well as some resources from the people who have proven themselves credible to me Whom I want to recognize:

Kaitlyn Young
Find me on Facebook at:
https://www.facebook.com/KaitlynmcSchasser

Check Out my personal contact site at:
https://aboutkaitlyn.phonesites.com

Join Our Mindset Group for "The Mind Ninja Company" At:
https://www.facebook.com/groups/371978274648230

Looking to Have your website or Conamazon.ctact info easily accessible?

I have a guy for that! Contact Joshua Luther at:

https://dynamiccards.net

Lastly, Please Make sure to Contact Wiley McArthur, This Dude can help you with your Mindset and business like no other.

https://themindninja.com or

Text "Ninja" to: 1-269-908-6479.

Made in United States
Orlando, FL
09 March 2022

15625511R00068